PRE-DECODABLE/ DE BOOKS
Take-Home Version

◆ Grade K ◆

Harcourt

Orlando   Boston   Dallas   Chicago   San Diego

Visit *The Learning Site!*
www.harcourtschool.com

PHOTO CREDITS:

I Am: bkcv, David A Northcott/SuperStock; ftcv, Tom Rosenthal/SuperStock; p.2, Chris McLaughlin/Corbisstockmarket; p.3, Stephen Krasemann/Photo Researchers Inc.; p.4, George Hunter/SuperStock; p.5, Harcourt; p.6, SuperStock; p.7, Renee Lynn/Photo Researchers Inc.

What Can Hop?: bkcv, ©ZEFA Germany/Corbisstockmarket; p.2, ©Peter Steiner/Corbisstockmarket; p.3, Renee Lynn/Photo Researchers Inc.; p.4, Terry Eggers/Corbisstockmarket; p.5, David A. Northcott/SuperStock; p.6, Mark A. Johnson/Corbisstockmarket; p.7, Tom McHugh/Steinhart Aquarium/Photo Researchers Inc.; p.8, Stephen Dalton/Photo Researchers Inc.

Contents

DECODABLE BOOKS

First Day at School

by Wendy Stillwell　　illustrated by Stephen Smock

Harcourt

------- Cut -------

2

------- Cut -------

8

3

- Cut - ✂

- Cut -

6

Cut

Where's My Teddy?

by Jane Simon   illustrated by Kevin O'Malley

Harcourt

--Cut--

2

----------------------- Cut -----------------------

8

3

- - - - - - - - - - - - Cut - - - - - - - - - - - -

School-Home Connection Have your child read the book to you.

4

- - - - - Cut - - - - - ✂

5

----- Cut -----

6

------ Cut ------

Pet Day

by Jane Simon   illustrated by Keiko Motoyama

- - - - - - Cut - - - - - -

a bear

7

a dog

2

--Cut--

a bear

8

a cat

3

- Cut -

 School-Home Connection Have your child read the book to you. Talk about pets you have or pets your child would like. Ask your child what it would be like to take that pet to school.

Word Count: 14
High-Frequency Word
a

a   fish

4

a mouse

5

6

Cut

My Bus

by John McWilliams   illustrated by Susan C. Calitri

Harcourt

- Cut -

my backpack

7

my socks

2

- Cut - ✂

my bus

8

my shoes

3

my jacket

4

------------------------------ Cut ------------------------------ ✂

my hat

5

- Cut -

my lunchbox

6

- Cut -

The Party

by Maryann Dobeck   illustrated by Lindy Burnett

Harcourt

- Cut -

the juice

7

the popcorn

2

---- Cut ----

the party!

8

the balloons

- - - - - - Cut -

 School-Home Connection Have your child list things needed to throw a party. Discuss why each item would be good for the party.

Word Count: 16
High-Frequency Words
   the
Story Word
   party

the pie

4

the milk

5

- Cut -

the hats

--Cut--✂

The Salad

by Ashley Riddle   illustrated by Liisa Chauncy Guida

Harcourt

- Cut -

I like onions.

7

I like carrots.

------------------------------ Cut ------------------------------ ✂

I like salad!

I like tomatoes.

3

-------------------------------- Cut --------------------------------

 School-Home Connection Have your child read the book to you, naming each vegetable that goes into the salad. Then ask him or her to name the first letter in each vegetable word.

Word Count: 23
High Frequency Words
 I
 like

I like peppers.

4

Harcourt
www.harcourtschool.com

I like lettuce.

5

I like celery.

6

-- Cut --

I Am

by Lisa Kindrey   illustrated by Stephanie Peterson

⬡Harcourt

- Cut -

I am orange.

I am blue.

2

- Cut -

8

I am red.

3

School-Home Connection Have your child read the book to you. Then name each color with your child and find an object in your home that is the same color.

Word Count: 20
High-Frequency Word
I

Decodable Word
am

PHOTO CREDITS
bkcv., David A. Northcott/SuperStock; ftcvr., Tom Rosenthal/SuperStock; pg. 2, Chris McLaughlin/Corbisstockmarket; pg. 3, Stephen Krasemann/Photo Researchers Inc.; pg. 4, George Hunter/SuperStock; pg. 5, Harcourt; pg. 6, SuperStock; pg. 7, Renee Lynn/Photo Researchers Inc.

I am green.

4

I am yellow.

5

‑ ‑ ‑ ‑ ‑ ‑ ‑ ‑ ‑ ‑ Cut ‑ ‑ ‑ ‑ ‑ ‑ ‑ ‑ ‑ ‑

I am purple.

6

- Cut - ✂

The Mat

by Kevin Kramer   illustrated by Rusty Fletcher

- Cut -

The elephant sat.

7

The mouse sat.

2

- Cut -

The mouse sat.

8

The snake sat.

3

School-Home Connection Have your child read the book to you. Ask your child to name the rainforest animals in the story. Then have your child name other rainforest animals that could have been used in the story.

Word Count: 23
High-Frequency Words   **Decodable Words**
  the   mat
                                       sat
                                       cat

The cat sat.

4

 The monkey sat.

- Cut -

The hippo sat.

6

- Cut - ✂

We Go

by Tim Pritchard   illustrated by Jane Chambers Wright

Harcourt

- Cut -

Raccoons go.

Bears go.

2

-- Cut --

We go.

8

Rabbits go.

3

----------------------------- Cut -----------------------------

 School-Home Connection Have your child read the book to you. Then have your child name different animals that live in the forest.

Word Count: 16
High-Frequency Words
    we
    go

 Deer go.

4

- Cut - ✂

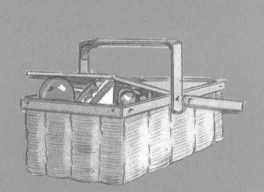

Skunks go.

5

Squirrels go.

- Cut - ✂

I Nap

by Geneeka Kazer   illustrated by Mary O'Keefe Young

Harcourt

------------------------------------ Cut ------------------------------------

2 ducklings nap.

5 kittens nap.

2

I nap.

8

3

------- Cut -------

 School-Home Connection Have your child read the book to you. Then go through the book one page at a time and have your child count the number of baby animals pictured.

Word Count: 12
High-Frequency Word
   I

Decodable Word
   nap

4 puppies nap.

4

- Cut - ✂

5

- Cut -

3 bunnies nap.

6

- Cut - ✂

Tap, Tap, Tap

by Kate Addison   illustrated by Kurt Nagahori

Harcourt

-- Cut --

Tap, tap, tap.

7

I am Rabbit.

2

---------------------------------- Cut ----------------------------------

I am Cat.

8

Tap, tap, tap.

3

-- Cut --

School-Home Connection Have your child read the book to you. Then ask him or her to name words that rhyme with tap, am, and cat.

Word Count: 24

High-Frequency Word
  I

Decodable Word
  tap
  am
  Cat

I am Skunk.

4

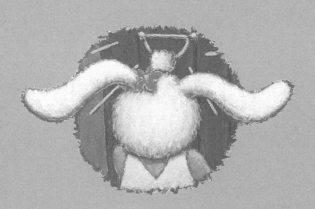

Tap, tap, tap.

5

- Cut -

I am Fox.

6

- Cut - ✂

The Park

by Linley Stover   illustrated by Paul Harvey

Harcourt

- Cut -

We go on a train.

We go to the park.

----- Cut -----

We like to go!

We go on a bus.

3

School-Home Connection Have your child read the book to you. Talk about your favorite things to do in the park.

Word Count: 36
High-Frequency Words

		Decodable Words
we	go	a
on	to	
the	like	

We go to the park.

4

- - - - Cut - - - - ✂

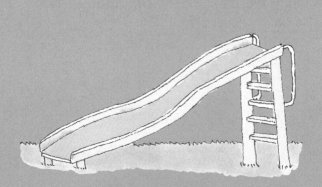

We go on a bike.

5

‐‐‐‐‐‐‐‐ Cut ‐‐‐‐‐‐‐‐

We go to the park.

6

------------------------- Cut -------------------------

Sit on My Chair

by Matthew Damon   illustrated by Wallace Keller

Harcourt

--- Cut ---

Sit on my pink chair.

7

Sit on my brown chair.

2

- Cut - ✂

I fit on my chair.

8

Sit on my red chair.

3

------------------------------ Cut ------------------------------

Word Count: 39

High-Frequency Words
  on
  my

Decodable Words
  sit

Sit on my blue chair.

4

- Cut - ✂

Harcourt
www.harcourtschool.com

Sit on my white chair.

5

------------------------------- Cut -------------------------------

Sit on my purple chair.

6

Cut

My Pig

by Lisa Masi   illustrated by Benrei Huang

Cut

My pig can paint.

My pig can run.

2

- Cut - ✂

My pig can hug.

8

My pig can jump.

3

------------------------------ Cut ------------------------------

School-Home Connection Have your child read the book to you. Then discuss with your child the things they can do now that they are in kindergarten.

Word Count: 30
High-Frequency Words
  my

Decodable Words
  pig
  can
  dig

My pig can draw.

4

Harcourt
www.harcourtschool.com

 My pig can dig.

5

 My pig can sing.

6

--- Cut ---

I Have, You Have

by Geneeka Kazer   illustrated by John B. Brunello

Harcourt

Cut

You have a boat.

7

I have a car.

--- Cut ---

We have a bike.

You have a car.

-- Cut --

School-Home Connection Have your child read the book to you. Then ask your child to name things to complete the sentences *I have a _____.* *You have a _____.*

....

Word Count: 32

High-Frequency Words	**Decodable Words**
have	I
you	a

I have a truck.

4

--- Cut ---

 You have a truck.

5

- Cut -

I have a boat.

6

----------------------------- Cut ----------------------------------✂

Soup

by Chris Bailey   illustrated by Scott A. Scheidly

Harcourt

------- Cut -------

Sip, sip, sip.

We have a pot.

2

-- Cut -- ✂

We like soup!

8

We have onions.

3

School-Home Connection Have your child read the book to you. Then ask your child to talk about favorite soups they would like to make.

Word Count: 24

High-Frequency Words
we
have
the
like

Decodable Words
a
lid
sip

We have carrots.

4

------------------------------Cut------------------------------ ✂

We have the lid.

5

We have cups.

6

The Dig

by Michelle DeCarlo   illustrated by Terri Chicko

Harcourt

- - - Cut - - -

We have the lid.

7

We have a map.

--- Cut ---

Jellybeans!

We have a shovel.

3

School-Home Connection Have your child read the book to you. Then ask your child to name words that rhyme with *map*, *dig*, and *lid*. Encourage him or her to try and spell each of the new words.

Word Count: 27

High-Frequency Words	Decodable Words
the	map
we	dig
have	a
	lid

We dig, dig, dig.

4

---- Cut ----

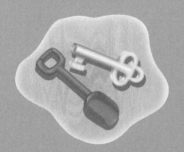

We have a box.

5

 We have a key.

6

Cut

Kip the Ant

by William O'Connor　　illustrated by Jim Durk

Harcourt

-- Cut --

Kip can tap.

What can Kip do?

-------------------------------- Cut --------------------------------✂

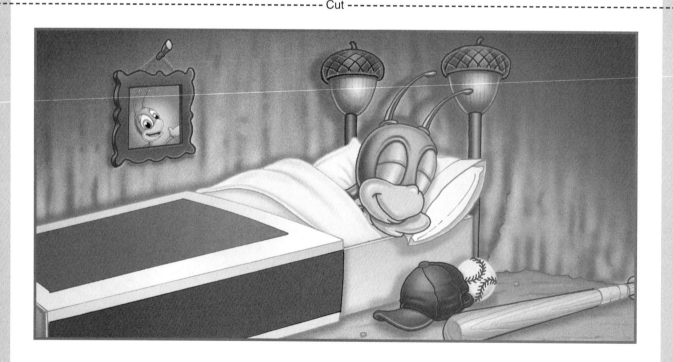

Kip can nap!

Kip can go.

3

------ Cut -------------------------------

School-Home Connection Have your child read the book to you. Then ask him or her to draw a picture of something else Kip might be able to do.

Word Count: 25
High-Frequency Words

the

what

do

go

Decodable Words

ant	dig
can	pat
Kip	tap
hit	nap

Kip can hit.

- Cut - ✂

Kip can dig.

- Cut -

Kip can pat.

6

- Cut - ✂

The Big Ram

by Petra Zubín   illustrated by Linda Bild

---- Cut ----

Can I go on top, Big Ram?

7

I am on top.

- Cut - ✂

I am on top!

Can I go on top, Big Ram?

3

--- Cut ---

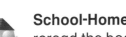

School-Home Connection Have your child read the book to you. Then reread the book and act it out, with one of you as the ram and the other as the caterpillar.

Word Count: 38

High-Frequency Words	**Decodable Words**	
the	big	top
go	ram	can
you	I	go
	am	not
	on	

You can not.

4

Can I go on top, Big Ram?

5

You can not.

6

Cut

What Can Hop?

by Lori Bedoski   illustrated by Sophia Latto

Can a frog hop?

7

A cat can not hop.

- Cut - ✂

It can hop!

A pig can not hop.

3

------ Cut ------

School-Home Connection Have your child read the book to you. Then talk about different animals and group them according to the way they move.

Word Count: 35
High-Frequency Word
what

Story Words
snake
frog

Decodable Words

can	a
cat	hop
not	pig
ram	bat
it	

PHOTO CREDITS
bkcv., c, ZEFA Germany/Corbisstockmarket; pg.2, c, Peter Steiner/Corbisstockmarket; pg.3, Renee Lynn/Photo Researchers Inc.; pg. 4, Terry Eggers/Corbisstockmarket; pg. 5, David A. Northcott/SuperStock; pg. 6, Mark A. Johnson/Corbisstockmarket; pg. 7, Tom McHugh/Steinhart Aquarium/Photo Researchers Inc.; pg. 8, Stephen Dalton/Photo Researchers Inc.

A ram can not hop.

4

A snake can not hop.

5

A bat can not hop.

6

- Cut -

I Can See It!

by Joan Miller   illustrated by Jeff Mack

Harcourt

- Cut -

You can sit on a box.

7

I can see a big top!

-------------------------------- Cut --------------------------------✂

I can see it!

I can see a man sit!

3

------------------------------ Cut ------------------------------

 School-Home Connection Have your child read the book to you. With your child, discuss the two boys in the story. Then ask your child to tell you how they are the same and how they are different.

Word Count: 42

High-Frequency Words

see   you

no

Decodable Words

I	can
a	big
top	man
not	sit
dog	it
on	box

I can see a dog sit!

4

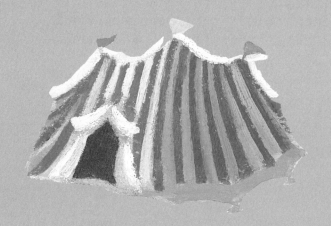

Can you see it?

- Cut -

No, I can not see it.

6

- Cut -

What Is in the Box?

by P. J. Casey   illustrated by Obadinah Heavner

Harcourt

No, it is not a fox.

Is a cat in the box?

-- Cut -- ✂

We see it.
A dog is in the box!

No, it is not a cat.

3

--- Cut ---

 School-Home Connection Have your child read the book to you. Then play a guessing game. Think of an object in the room and give your child clues about it. For example: I'm thinking of something whose name rhymes with *cook*. (book)

Word Count: 50

High-Frequency Words

what	see
the	we
no	

Decodable Words

is	a
in	cat
box	not
pig	fox
it	dog

Is a pig in the box?

4

No, it is not a pig.

-------------------------------- Cut ---------------------------------

Is a fox in the box?

------- Cut -------

Hop on Top

by Carlos Velasquez   illustrated by Loreen Leedy

Harcourt

-----------------------✂ Cut -----------------------

Hop on top, Fox.

My cap is on top.
Can you tap it, Pop?

-- Cut -- ✂

I got it! I got my cap!

I can not.

- Cut -

 School-Home Connection Have your child read the book to you. Then write the word *hop* on a piece of paper. Ask your child to make new words by changing one letter in the word. Then take turns making and reading new words.

Word Count: 44

High-Frequency Words	Decodable Words	
my	hop	cap
you	I	Fox
on	it	tap
	can	not
	got	is
	Pop	top

My cap is on top.
Can you tap it, Mom?

4

------------------------------ Cut ------------------------------

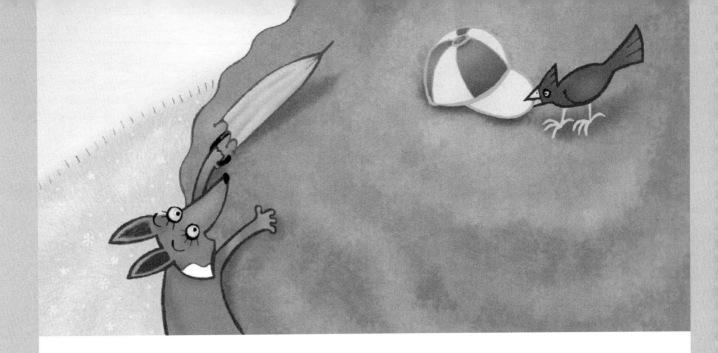

I can not.

5

✂ - Cut -

Hop on top, Mom.

6

- Cut -

A Big, Big Van

by Joyce Carol   illustrated by Marvin Eldridge

Harcourt

- - - - - - - - - - - - - - - - - - - Cut - - - - - - - - - - - - - - - - - - -

Come, Sal. Look in the box.

7

I can see a big, big van.

--- Cut ---

I can pat a big, big cat!

Come, Pam. Look at the van.

3

School-Home Connection Have your child read the book to you. Then have your child draw a picture of a pet he or she would like to get and label the picture with the pet's name.

Word Count: 48

High-Frequency Words

see
come
look
the

Decodable Words

a	big	I
can	Pam	at
at	van	Dan
in	box	Sal
pat	cat	is
Dad		

Dad is in the van.

4

Come, Dan. Look in the van.

5

Cut

I can see a big, big box.

6

Come In

by Jane Cassidy   illustrated by Paige Billin-Frye

Cut

Do not come in, Max.
A dog can not come in.

It is hot, Ron.
Come in to get wet.

- Cut - ✂

Max is not hot!

Come in, Meg.
It is not hot in the pool.

3

---- Cut ----

School-Home Connection Have your child read the book to you. Then have your child think of rhyming words for each of the names. For example, your child might say *Jen-men*; *Meg-peg*.

Word Count: 61

High-Frequency Words

come
look
do
to
the

Decodable Words

in	it	is
hot	Ron	can
get	wet	Meg
Jim	Pat	at
a	Max	not
dog		

Story Word

pool

It is hot, Jim.
Come in to get wet.

4

Come in, Pat.
It is not hot in the pool.

5

- Cut -

Look at Max.
Max is hot.

6

Hop In!

by Rob Arego   illustrated by Laura Ovresat

Harcourt

- - - - - - - - - - - - - - - - Cut - - - - - - - - - - - - - - - -

My van can not go.
What can I do?

My van can go.

- Cut - ✂

You can go!

Hop in my van, Pam.
Get in, Nat.

3

------------------------------ Cut ------------------------------

School-Home Connection Have your child read the book to you. Then have your child draw a picture of his or her favorite animal in the van and label the drawing by writing *A _____ is in a van.*

Word Count: 50

High-Frequency Words	**Decodable Words**	
do	van	can
go	Jed	I
my	Pam	in
the	Bev	Lil
to	Dot	Jon
what	hop	get
you	not	Tim

Hop in my van, Bev.
Get in, Jed.

4

Harcourt
www.harcourtschool.com

Hop in my van, Lil.
Get in, Tim.

- Cut -

Hop in my van, Dot.
Get in, Jon.

6

Is It for Me?

by Jodi Lee   illustrated by Laura Freeman

Harcourt

-----✂ - Cut -

Yes, it is.

It is a red box.
Is it for me?

2

------------------------------ Cut ------------------------------ ✂

It is for me.
It is a cap!

8

No, it is not.

3

------- Cut -------

School-Home Connection Have your child read the book to you. Ask your child to write another story ending in which he or she receives a box in the mail. Help your child write one or two sentences about what is in the box.

Word Count: 50

High-Frequency Words
- for
- me
- no

Decodable Words
is	it
a	red
box	not
big	tan
yes	cap

It is a big box.
Is it for me?

4

---Cut---

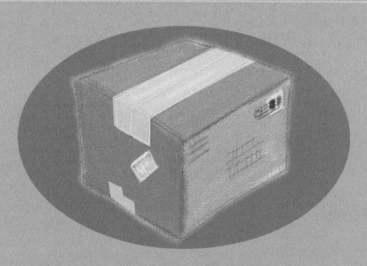

No, it is not.

5

It is a tan box.
Is it for me?

- Cut - ✂

We Can Fix

by Michael O'Toole   illustrated by Pamela Eklund

Harcourt

- Cut -

I can fix a net.
Nip, nip, nip.

7

I can fix a bed.
Tap, tap, tap.

2

--------------------------------- Cut ---------------------------------

We can fix it!

8

I can fix a pet.
Pat, pat, pat.

3

 School-Home Connection Have your child read the book to you. Talk with your child about other people who have jobs fixing things in your neighborhood.

....

Word Count: 55

High-Frequency Word

we

Decodable Words

can	fix	it
I	a	bed
tap	pet	pat
van	rap	rip
zip	top	dab
net	nip	

I can fix a van.
Rap, rap, rap.

4

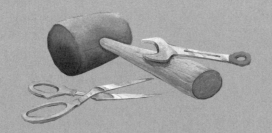

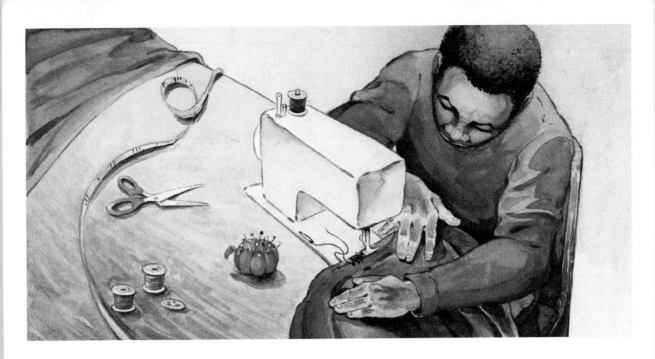

I can fix a rip.
Zip, zip, zip.

5

I can fix a top.
Dab, dab, dab.

6

Cut

A Hat I Like

by William James   illustrated by Rob Hefferan

Harcourt

Cut

Not yet, Nan.

I see a hat I like, Dad.
Can I get a hat like it?

2

------------------------------- Cut -------------------------------

You can get a hat like me!

8

Not yet, Jen.

- Cut -

 School-Home Connection Have your child read the book to you. Talk about different community workers in your neighborhood and what they do.

Word Count: 60

High-Frequency Words

like	see
me	look
the	you

Decodable Words

a	hat	Dad
can	I	get
it	not	yet
Jen	Mom	Ted
Nan		

Look at the hat, Mom. Can I get a hat like it?

4

Cut

Not yet, Ted.

5

--------------------------------- Cut ---------------------------------

I see a hat I like, Dad.
Can I get a hat like it?

6

----------- Cut -----------

Little Cat, Big Cat

by Laura Black   illustrated by Paul Yalowitz

Harcourt

Cut

It is him!
Do you have a net, Fox?

7

I am sad, Pig.
Did you see Little Cat?

-------- Cut --------

I have one, Big Cat.
I can get him.

I did not, Big Cat.
Did Dog see him?

3

-- Cut --

 School-Home Connection Have your child read the book to you. Then talk about another way that Big Cat could have gotten Little Cat down from the tree. Have your child draw a picture of it.

Word Count: 67

High-Frequency Words		Decodable Words	
little	you	cat	I
see	have	sad	pig
one	do	not	big
		dog	fox
		can	it
		him	a
		is	am
		get	did
		net	

I am sad, Dog.
Did you see Little Cat?

4

- Cut -

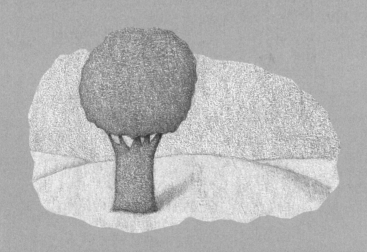

Harcourt
www.harcourtschool.com

I did not, Big Cat.
Did Fox see him?

5

I am sad, Fox.
Did you see Little Cat?

6

------------------------------------ Cut ------------------------------------

But I Can

by Sinda Sweeny   illustrated by Sheila Bailey

Harcourt

Cut

Max can not cut, but I can.

7

Max is little. I am big.

-------------------------------- Cut --------------------------------

I am big. Max is little.
I can not fit, but Max can!

Max can not hop, but I can.

3

------ Cut ------

School-Home Connection Have your child reread the book to you. Talk about the things your child can do now that he or she couldn't do before.

Word Count: 58

High-Frequency Word
little

Decodable Words

but	I
Max	is
am	hop
get	run
it	hit
can	fit
big	cut
not	

Max can not run, but I can.

4

- Cut - ✂

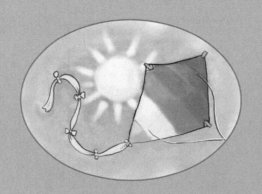

Max can not get it, but I can.

--- Cut ---

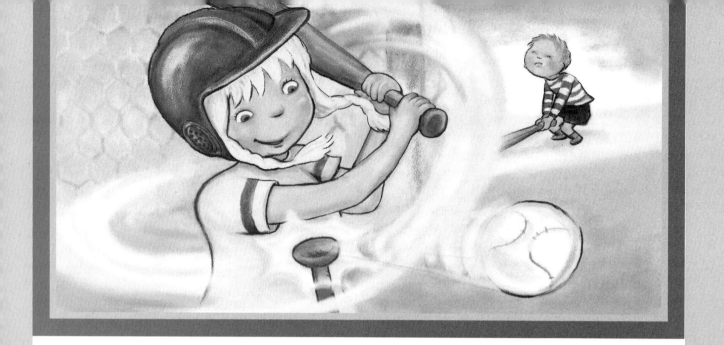

Max can not hit, but I can.

6

Cut

Up, Up, Up

by Asa Spahn   illustrated by Roberta Collier-Morales

Harcourt

I see a fat cub nap.
Look at it nap, nap, nap.

I go up, up, up.
What do I see?

2

------------------------------------ Cut ------------------------------------

I am at the top.
I see a big sun set.

8 Look at it set, set, set.

I see a red fox run.
Look at it run, run, run.

3

School-Home Connection Have your child read the book to you. Then have your child choose his or her favorite animal and find out more information about it.

Word Count: 89

High-Frequency Words

go	what
do	see
look	little
the	

Decodable Words

up	I	a
red	fox	run
at	it	big
sip	tan	hop
fat	cub	nap
am	top	sun
set		

I see a little bird tap.
Look at it tap, tap, tap.

4

-- Cut --

I see a big deer sip.
Look at it sip, sip, sip.

5

I see a tan rabbit hop.
Look at it hop, hop, hop.

6

------ Cut ------

Is It a Fish?

by Trent Brekard   illustrated by JoAnn Adinolfi

Cut

Tug, tug, tug.
Is it a fish?

Here we are!
Get a rod.

2

--Cut--

Come look.
See what Jen got.
It is a big fish!

8

Tug, tug, tug.
Is it a fish?
No, it is a man! **3**

------------------------------- Cut -------------------------------

....

Word Count: 78

High-Frequency Words

here	are
come	see
we	no
look	what

Decodable Words

is	it	a
get	rod	tug
man	did	Mom
bug	hen	Ted
jug	Jen	got
big		

Tug, tug, tug.
Did Mom get a fish?
4   No, it is a bug!

- Cut - ✂

Tug, tug, tug.
Is it a fish?
No, it is a hen!

5

Tug, tug, tug.
Did Ted get a fish?
6   No, it is a jug!

It Is Fun

by Michelle Lawrence   illustrated by Julia Gorton

Harcourt

- - - - - - Cut - - - - - -

I do not like it, Pam.
It is not fun.

7

Come on, Sam.
It is fun here.

I like it a lot.

----------------------------- Cut -----------------------------

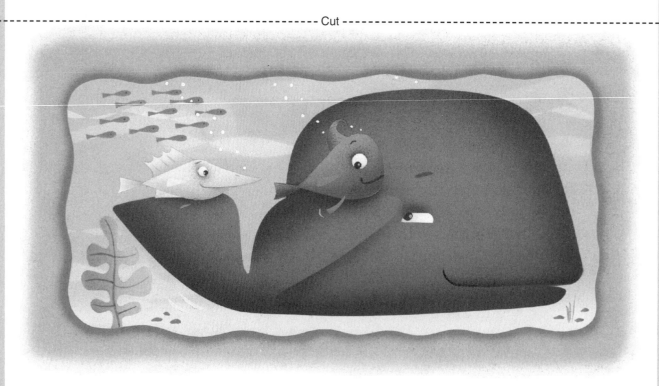

I like it, Pam.
It is fun here.

I do not like it, Pam.
It is not fun.

3

School-Home Connection Have your child read the book to you. Then talk about different animals that live under the sea. Have your child choose one, draw a picture of it, and write its name beneath it.

Word Count: 71
High-Frequency Words

come	the
here	see
like	do
look	

Decodable Words

it	is
on	Sam
a	lot
at	bug
net	Pam
fun	I
not	

Look at the bug, Sam.
See, it is fun.

4

I do not like it, Pam.
It is not fun.

5

Look at the net, Sam.
See, it is fun.

6

- Cut - ✂

A Bug Can Tug

by Maxine Dunhill   illustrated by Carly Castillon

Harcourt

- - - - - Cut - - - - -

I am little, but my boat is big.

7

My boat can not go.
I did not get gas.
I can not fix it.

2

----- Cut -----

A bug can tug!

8

 Cat, can you tug me?

 I can not tug you, Dog.

My boat is not big. **3**

- Cut -

Word Count: 89

High-Frequency Words

my
go
you
me
little

Story Word

boat

Decodable Words

a	bug	can
tug	not	I
fix	it	Cat
is	big	Pig
Fox	Dog	am
but	get	did
gas		

Pig, can you tug me?

I can not tug you, Dog.

My boat is not big.

4

------- Cut -------

 Fox, can you tug me?

 I can not tug you, Dog.

My boat is not big.　　5

- Cut -

 I can tug you, Dog.
A bug can not tug.

6

Cut ----------------

Sid Hid

by Tim Buckwalter   illustrated by Reggie Holladay

- Cut -

Did you look in his little shell?

I did not.

7

 Sid hid.
I can not see him.

--- Cut ---

 Sid is in it.
Sid is in his shell!

 Did you look in the big box?
I did. Sid is not in it.

3

School-Home Connection Have your child read the book to you. Then talk about the different underwater creatures. Talk about how they are alike and how they are different.

Word Count: 84

High-Frequency Words
see
you
look
the
little

Story Word
shell

Decodable Words

Sid	hid
can	not
did	in
box	is
red	bag
can	big
his	I
him	big
it	tin
pot	

 Did you look in the red bag?

I did. Sid is not in it.

4

Did you look in the tin can?

I did. Sid is not in it.

5

- Cut -

Did you look in the big pot?

I did. Sid is not in it.

6

----- Cut -----

In a Sub

by John McNamara   illustrated by Pamela Johnson

Harcourt

- - - - - - - - - - - - - - - - - Cut - - - - - - - - - - - - - - - - -

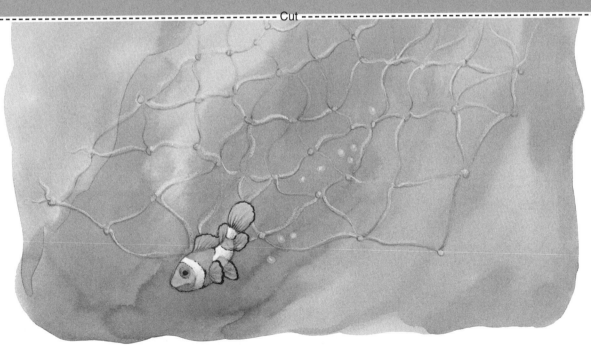

Look at the fish!
It is not in a net.

I am in a sub.
What can I see?

2

-------------------------------- Cut --------------------------------

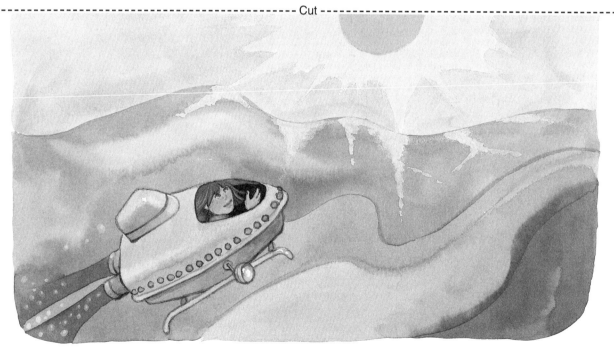

I go up in a sub.
I can see the sun.
8   I had fun!

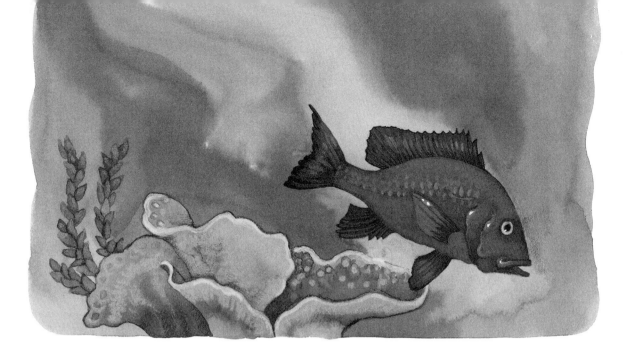

Look! It is a red fish.
It can zip. Go, red fish!

3

------------------------------- Cut -------------------------------

School-Home Connection Have your child read the book to you. Then work with your child to write captions about each of the underwater creatures.

Word Count: 87

High-Frequency Words

what	see
look	go
you	the

Decodable Words

in	a	sub
can	I	red
zip	at	it
big	has	fin
not	dig	is
net	up	sun
am	fit	had
fun	tip	

Story Words

fish	shark
crab	clam

It is a shark!
It has a big fin.
4   Can you see the tip?

- - - - - - - - - - Cut - - - - - - - - - - ✂

It is a crab.
It can dig.
Look at it go!

5

It is a clam.

The clam is little.

6 I can not fit in it.